John Henry Walsh

Spiral Plan of teaching Arithmetic

John Henry Walsh

Spiral Plan of teaching Arithmetic

ISBN/EAN: 9783337165871

Printed in Europe, USA, Canada, Australia, Japan

Cover: Foto ©Paul-Georg Meister /pixelio.de

More available books at **www.hansebooks.com**

I. THE SPIRAL METHOD.

II. WHAT IS NEEDED IN AN IDEAL
TEXT BOOK.

III. PLAN AND SCOPE OF THE WALSH
BOOKS.

I.

THE SPIRAL METHOD.

A brief description of one or more typical text-books of the old style will enable the reader to realize the fundamental defects of those made after that plan. **The Old-time Text-book.**

The author of a book of that class fails to understand that the logical development of the subject matter produces almost invariably a faulty arrangement of topics to be followed by the young pupil. The result of his labors may be a good book of reference, but a bad teaching book.

In the old grammars, the first place was given to an explanation of the word "grammar," then one of "English grammar." This was followed by the enumeration of the four parts, and a definition of each. Next in order would come the elaboration of the first part, covering many · pages. The very young pupil was expected to learn that "orthography treats of letters, syllables, separate words, and spelling;" after which the classification of the letters was given. Vowels and consonants (with the double-barreled *w* and *y*), mutes and liquids, labials, dentals, etc., would help to befog the youthful intellect. **Grammar.**

However, the student's troubles were only beginning. Although he might know the declensions, comparisons and conjugations almost as well as the teacher, he didn't know that he knew them, nor was he taught how to study them. Blindly he struggled for many weary months, and with what result? Possibly he became able to repeat many meaningless forms.

Geography.

A geography text-book almost invariably began with a definition of "geography," then stated the division of the subject into mathematical, physical, political, etc., with the definition of each. Although mathematical geography is the least interesting, as well as the most difficult, for the beginner, it had to be completed before the next division was touched; and so on with the remaining divisions.

Spelling-book.

The arrangement of the speller was frequently according to the number of syllables in the word—monosyllables taking the first place, followed by disyllables, trisyllables, etc., utterly regardless of the needs of the pupil. If homonyms were included, they came late in the book and were arranged alphabetically. The child could not learn the difference between *to*, *two*, and *too*, until he had worried through the unfamiliar words under the earlier letters—cygnet and signet, crewel and cruel, fane and feign, for instance.

Arithmetic.

In arithmetic, after definitions of *quantity*, *unit*, *number*, *concrete*, *abstract*, etc., the subject of numeration and notation was reached. When the author deemed this sufficiently exhausted—some books go up to twenty periods, vigintillions—he took up addition, not forgetting, however, to give several principles and rules in the first topic. Addition had its definitions, principles, and rules, and a more or less exhaustive treatment. Then came subtraction, multiplication, and division, each containing its set of definitions,

principles, and rules, and each being practically completed before the next was begun. This work generally filled up four years, all through which many un-
fortunates were compelled for various reasons to leave
school.

Before the sacred ground of fractions could be trod-
den, a probationary period had to be spent among the
"properties of numbers," which gave the author an
opportunity to tax the child mind with a lot of things
about prime numbers and composite numbers, and
composite numbers prime to each other; with factors
and multiples, and common factors; with common
divisors and greatest common divisors; with common
multiples and least common multiples. Each new
name had its definition, which made it no clearer; each
subdivision had its principles and rules; each had its
set of examples—with possibly a few heart-breaking
problems.

The subject of fractions afforded rare ground for
the old-time author and his modern follower. Definitions were given of *fraction, fractional unit, unit of the
fraction, numerator, denominator, common fraction, proper fraction, improper fraction, simple fraction, compound fraction, complex fraction and mixed number.*
Before the pupil was permitted to add ½ and ½, he
had to be taught how to reduce a whole number to an
improper fraction, and a mixed number to an improper
fraction; a simple fraction to lowest terms, to higher
terms, and to given higher terms; fractions to equivalent fractions with the least common denominator; and
compound fractions to simple fractions.

Sufficient has been given to show the dreariness of
the old text-book, especially in the hands of a teacher

who required the memorizing of each definition, principle and rule; although the gradual development of the subject in a "logical" order might delight an aged philosopher. It is difficult, however, to defend a scheme of instruction that would prevent a pupil from seeing in a text-book how to find the cost of a half of a 10 cent pie until he had been at school nearly six years; or the method of calculating how much would have to be paid for a pint of milk when it sold for 6 cents a quart, until he had spent still another year in the study of arithmetic.

The Two-book Series. When the author of this style of text-book decided that a two-book series was advisable, he did not change the "logical" arrangement. All of the sins of the higher book generally appeared in the lower one, and in an aggravated form because of the condensation necessary to make a smaller book. To obtain as many purchasers as possible, the first book of arithmetic contained nearly all the topics of the higher . one, but with many fewer examples for practice.

Reform in Text-books. The German educators were probably the first to realize the defects of the old-time text-book, although the German pupil suffered comparatively little from its use, owing to the slight dependence of his teacher upon the book. When, however, it was found that the study of grammar did not result in any lessening of the number of mistakes made by a pupil in speaking or in writing, the intelligent teacher came to understand that correctness in speaking and in writing comes from long-continued practice in correct speaking and writing, that many people are correct in these respects, who have never studied technical grammar, and that many others, able to repeat glibly all of the rules of syntax with their exceptions, habitually blunder. It is now admitted that the science of grammar is of no use in bringing pupils to correct habits of speech, that all it can do is to help training in thought. In the elementary school it has no place except in the highest classes, and there for its disciplinary rather than for its practical value.

To give the required practice in correct talking and writing, it became necessary to develop a systematic series of language lessons intended to lead pupils to the employment of the proper forms. In these lessons the "spiral" arrangement was necessarily adopted, each year getting its share in drills in the correct use of the common irregular verbs, for instance, and in speaking and writing correctly the sentences likely to contain mistakes in default of such practice. No fear of disturbing the "logical" order of topics prevents the maker of a course of study in language from prescribing such lessons for pupils of even the lowest grades as will bring their "Him and me done it" into something more in accordance with the best usage. He considers the arrangement of the subject matter from the standpoint of the proper training of the child, and leaves the "logical" arrangement for books of reference or for text-books used by students of some maturity. *"Spiral" Language Lessons.*

The modern geography is gradually dropping its thought-depressing definitions. Children are led to getting accurate notions of land and water forms without being compelled to memorize set collections of words, to them meaningless. The subject is led up to, before the text-book is reached, in systematic oral lessons through the lower classes. A new elementary geography goes over the whole ground three times in *"Spiral" Geography* the one book, adding a few more details in the second treatment, and still more in the third.

"Spiral" Spelling. The winner of the prize at an old time spelling-match was frequently unable to write a short letter without making some orthographical blunders. The new graded speller, besides providing for much practice in writing words correctly, has so changed the old arrangement as to teach children to use "their" or "there" properly before the letter t is reached in the homonym subdivision. Each series of lessons now has its proper share of the things that should be taught a child likely to leave school before the middle of the book is studied.

"Spiral" Arithmetic. Text-books in arithmetic have been somewhat slow in responding to the demand for modern improvements. Owing to the fact that books are not placed in the hands of pupils of graded schools until they are nearly half through the elementary course, superintendents were able to effect many changes for the better in the lower classes. Pupils of these grades have been required during the first school year to solve oral problems involving any of the four fundamental operations, and even to find fractional parts of small numbers. The more commonly used denominate units were brought into the work of these grades, and many other valuable reforms were made. The authors, in self-defense, were compelled to re-write their first books; but the majority of them have left in the second books all of the old, old faults.

The result has been to handicap the superintendents of schools in a great measure. A good course in the work of the first four years, with the details carefully elaborated, is followed in the fifth year with

the requirement that Blank's Arithmetic be studied
from page — to page —. A similar one is made for
the remaining years.

It is time for children to begin to use books, if they
have not had them before, and it is inadvisable to suggest too much flitting about from one part of the book
to another. In this way, pupils that have multiplied
by a mixed number in the lower grades, and worked
simple problems involving pounds and ounces, pecks
and bushels, are compelled to drop these topics entirely until the "logical" order brings them again into
view. The pupils are not even permitted, in this respect, to "mark time;" they must retreat, through the
failure of the books to furnish ammunition.

As an illustration of the "spiral" method in history, **"Spiral"**
a plan followed in good schools may be shown in a few **Method in**
Teaching
words. Before the regular text-book is reached, the **History.**
subject is taught orally, being commenced in the lower
grades with stories about historical personages. The
idea is to cover the whole period of American history
as frequently as possible. The first year's pupils are
told about, say, Columbus, John Smith, Washington,
Lincoln, and McKinley. The next class is told about
or reads about the same persons with additional
details, and other characters are introduced, say,
De Soto, Penn, Putnam, Grant, Dewey. In a city
system in which free books are supplied, a short bio-
graphical history is taken up and read in a year. The
next year another is read and discussed, all this being
done before history is taken up as a formal study.

The foregoing method, while offensive to the person
who would prefer to stick to one book divided chron-
ologically into as many periods as there were classes

studying history, is probably traceable to the French plan of "concentric courses."

After their defeat by the Prussians, which the French attributed largely to the superior education of their opponents, they resolved to spare neither money nor effort to increase the efficiency of their schools of all kinds to the greatest possible extent. They have expended enormous sums of money in equipping the schools and in obtaining the best obtainable talent to teach and to direct the teaching. Under these circumstances, it is not strange that the French schools during the past twenty-five years have forged ahead more rapidly than those of any other country of the world.

The striking feature of the French system is the organization of the studies of the elementary schools into three "concentric courses" of two years each, the pupils of these six years corresponding approximately to our classes from the third year to the eighth, inclusive. The first two years are spent in the "maternal school," in which the teaching is chiefly oral; but during the other six years text-books in reading, language, geography, history and arithmetic are used. In each of the last four subjects a different book is taken up every second year, each book covering the whole subject, but in a method adapted to the capacity of the student. The "spiral" arrangement in France is more properly called the "concentric circle" method.

II.

WHAT IS NEEDED IN AN IDEAL TEXT-BOOK.

To determine the requirements of a good teaching book, or series of books, for elementary schools, two things must be determined. One has been alluded to previously—the proper arrangement of the subject matter from the standpoint of the learner, which is almost the opposite of the "logical" arrangement desirable in a book of reference.

The other is the careful consideration of the arrangement that will best take care of the proper development and training of the too large number of unfortunate children driven from school at all stages of the course through poverty or other misfortune. Two-thirds of the school children are found in the classes of the first four years, and nearly one-third are in the classes of the second four years. The number in the high schools constitute fewer than one-fiftieth, while the number in college constitutes but an inappreciable fraction.

Arrangement of Subject Matter.

Short School Life of Many Pupils.

The following figures taken from a recent report of a city school system show the number per thousand of pupils on register in classes of each school year from the first to the twelfth. As tuition, text-books, and supplies of every kind are furnished free of cost, the showing is more favorable as to length of school life than is likely to obtain in cities less favored and in the rural districts.

Primary classes	1st year	185	
	2d "	173	
	3d "	159	
	4th "	144	661 total
Grammar classes	5th "	125	
	6th , "	93	
	7th "	58	
	8th "	35	311 "
High school classes	9th "	16	
	10th "	7	
	11th "	4	
	12th "	1	28 "
			1000 "

While it is impossible for the average person to draw accurate conclusions from the foregoing figures they show nevertheless a constant dropping-out of those that need all our assistance. If a superintendent could be sure of keeping all his pupils 12 years or 8 years or even 4 years, he could so arrange his course of study as to give a certain completeness to the education received up to that time. The problem, however, is somewhat more difficult, especially as the short school life of too many is interrupted by frequent absences from various causes.

The system that provides for only those that go to the high school is doing a very small share of its proper work.

The ideal text-book, therefore, must contain such an arrangement of its subject matter as will give something substantial at as many points in the course as possible.

The book that takes up each topic as frequently as possible helps out the school life of its user by making it easier to promote the boy or girl that is a little "below grade" because of enforced absence or of the possession of fewer brains than the other pupils. In the use of the old time book, a pupil that had failed to master a topic had no chance to review it properly; the user of the ideal book should have several opportunities.

Ideal Book vs. Topical One.

The maker of a good text-book must not be too radical. The method given in the previous chapter, of reading history by covering the whole ground each year or two, is not applicable, at least in all of its details, in a text-book of arithmetic. While a boy can easily understand all about Dewey, although the latter belongs in the last chapter of a chronological history, and while he is likely to be as much interested in the hero of Manila Bay as in the Northmen of the first chapter, the same is not true of cube root as compared with addition. The early curves of the arithmetic "spiral" should not include too many topics, nor ones too advanced. Some authors, finding the "spiral" method a good one, have carried it to too great extremes. Having convinced themselves that they have discovered an ingenious method of simplifying an advanced topic, they work it into an early page of their books. They forget, however, that the important thing to do for every pupil of the common school is to give him, at the earliest possible moment, a working familiarity with the fundamental processes, the ability to use simple fractions in their commoner applications, and some acquaintance with the solution of problems involving the most commonly used denominate units. To permit the child to fritter away valuable

Selection of Topics.

Mistakes of some Authors.

time on less important matters, at the risk of failing to obtain the essentials, is an educational crime.

Measurements, Percentage and Interest

On the other hand, it is unwise to allow the scholar of the fifth and sixth years to give his whole time to tiresome drills in fractions, decimals and denominate numbers to the exclusion of even elementary lessons in measurements, percentage, and interest. It is possible to give these by the end of the sixth year, or a little earlier; and no child should be deprived of this much arithmetic, who is forced through poverty to give up attendance at school before taking up the work of the seventh year. The boy or girl able to remain longer will obtain a better knowledge of these topics; but the others should receive at least some instruction therein.

Omission of Non-essentials.

In considering what should be contained in the ideal book, it must not be forgotten that judicious omissions constitute a source of strength in a teaching arithmetic. There was a time when the author of a geography prided himself upon the multitude of details that were crowded into his maps; to-day he calls attention to their small number. Arithmetic is studied to develop mathematical power in the learner, and not to give him a mass of isolated facts; and the more the pupil's attention is distracted by the latter, the less likelihood there is that he will obtain the full benefit to be derived from the study. A boy that is "good at figures" can readily adapt himself to the arithmetical requirements of almost any calling, as soon as he learns the few facts peculiar to his position.

Ability to work examples involving denominate numbers can be very much better obtained from the use of a few tables containing familiar units, than from the introduction of the other tables. The absence of the "related predicates" in the case of the latter, tends very much to the confusion of the youthful learner. Meeting a new table a few years later in a new business gives him no trouble, because the daily routine furnishes the "related predicates" that are not present in his school days.

Many books prevent the pupil from testing his powers. Each topic or subdivision of a topic is treated as if it were something entirely new; and explanations, principles and rules are furnished where their introduction is a positive injury to the learner's development. The older authors were content to give only four sets of rules, after they had reached addition of fractions; some newer ones work in at least two more: "To find what fractional part one number is of another," and "To find the whole when the fractional part is given." *Unnecessary Explanations and Rules.*

Probably the worst teaching done in our schools occurs in the arithmetic classes in the seventh year. At this stage, percentage is generally reached; and at a time when some mathematical power should have been gained, the author and teacher endeavor to prevent its display. The only new thing in percentage that the thirteen-year-old pupil needs to know before being set to work at the exercises, is the meaning of the term "per cent." Being told that, he should be able to solve every question that does not contain any strange technical words. The pupil has solved similar problems in the fifth year in fractions, and in the sixth year in decimals; and it would seem a pedagogical blunder to force unnecessary assistance *Bad Teaching of Percentage.*

upon him, were it not an offence committed by authors of high repute.

Unnecessary Subdivisions. Not content with stifling all growth at the outset of the new topic by their wrong treatment of it, these authors present the same thing again and again under such new names as insurance, commission, brokerage, profit and loss, taxes, duties, and apparently endeavor to prevent a scholar from ascertaining that he is not taking up something strange by giving him a set of rules, principles, and cases, with each subdivision. A boy or girl would be positively benefited by the omission from the text book of every one of these sub-topics. This would not prevent a teacher from giving problems usually placed under one or other subdivisions if she were careful to avoid the introduction of unfamiliar words, whose meaning could not readily be determined from the context. Any other examples are unnecessary. The well-taught pupil can handle any he meets in his particular business.

Because of the meagerness of the results obtained from the study of arithmetic, some well-meaning peda- **New-fangled Systems of Arithmetic.** gogues have assumed that the present methods are wrong, root and branch. Instead of endeavoring to improve the present system by the needed reforms, they begin with the assumption that nothing is right. They wish to kill the rats by burning the barn, a rather wasteful procedure. The Grube method was the first, in recent years, to obtain any wide-spread acceptance. The good things in this method are still employed in a modified way; but the interminable grind prescribed by its author is not now carried out by any sane teacher.

Two new methods, each guaranteed to be a specific

for all the mathematical ills we suffer, have recently **The Rational** been proposed in all seriousness.   The first assumes **Method.** that failure to teach arithmetic properly is due to the adherence of teachers to the "fixed unit" of the Grube system.   If the current practice of the schools were to begin work in number with an elaborate drill on the number one, there might be some reason for writing an article to show the absurdity of such procedure; but as no teacher does anything of the kind, the author of the "movable unit" method is threshing the air.   If teachers were bound to inflict upon babes tiresome drills on the "unit," it would be well to suggest the employment of the "movable" one; but as teachers, in the main, are rational beings, they will not worry about either variety of unit.   How ridiculous it is to waste energy in teaching children what they know already; or what they will inevitably learn without teaching, and learn better.   What need to drill elaborately on the facts that 1 cent is different from 1 nickel, that 1 hour is not 1 day, etc., etc.   The only new things introduced into the teaching of arithmetic by the author of the "Rational method" are the worse than useless ones of obscuring the terms of a straight-forward problem by the introduction of references to his "movable" units.   The text-book written to exploit the method would be vastly improved by the omission of every reference thereto.   It contains many good things, but they are all old; what is new in it is bad (for teaching purposes).

The zealous introducer of the "ratio" method **The "Ratio'** points with pride to the wonderful results produced by **Method.** the use of his system, with its elaborate outfit of splints, squares, rectangles, triangles, cubes, prisms, cones, and what not. The same remarkable things are claimed by each inventor of something new in education. Some of the lookers-on are deluded into the belief that the philosopher's stone has been found at last. Others, more experienced, understand that children can be taught anything; but they realize that the price paid may be the irreparable injury of the children. Bright teachers, proud of the advertising they get from streams of visitors, and desirous of obtaining the commendation of their superiors, will fail to appreciate the harm they are doing their young charges by prematurely forcing them into tasks beyond their years. The complicated ratios introduced by this system into the number work of the lowest years, will inevitably do much harm to the development of immature minds. What is sought of the babe can be obtained much better if postponed until the proper time.

Too much Machinery. One thing that will inevitably militate against the success of a method requiring too much machinery in its operations is the failure of the over-burdened teacher to employ the necessary material, even when it is supplied, and the unwillingness of the school authorities to continue to furnish supplies that are kept unused in dark closets. While teachers in city schools, having only pupils of a single grade, may struggle for a time with the method, it cannot possibly meet with any favor at the hands of teachers having pupils of more than one grade. The very best results in objective teaching are generally found in the classes in which the objective material is obtained through efforts of the teacher or pupils. Home-made apparatus of nearly every kind is much more effective in class work than that supplied by school boards.

It is not so much a new method of teaching arith- Science of
metic that is needed, as a modification of existing Arithmetic
methods. In the first place, teachers must understand Computing.
that babes have no business with the *science* of number;
the main object during the early school years should
be to teach the *art* of computing. This makes unnecessary all definitions and principles. When notation
and numeration are taught beginners, there should be
no wasteful elaboration of method of showing the value
of the figure in the tens' place or of the one in the
hundreds' place, the bundles of ten splints and the
larger ones of a hundred splints. Young children can
learn to read and write 39 without much trouble; all
the time spent in endeavoring to give them an adequate
notion of 39 is thrown away. The little parrots can
be made to say anything the teacher wishes them to
say; they can learn to manipulate the single splints and
the bundles of ten; but the speeches and the per-
formance are meaningless to the baby actors, although
their teacher does not always realize it.

When written addition is to be taught, the teacher The "how",
should show his pupils the "how" of the carrying, not not the
the "why." This is the opinion of all the soundest "why."
educators of our country, even if it disagrees with the
practice of the girl whose normal-school diploma is a
few months old. While she may think the children
know what they are talking about, when they glibly
rattle off the unmeaning formulas prescribed by her,
she is seriously deluding herself. It is not claimed, of
course, that children are much injured by this simple
teacher's methods; a kind Providence has ordained
that the infantile mind does not waste much effort in
the endeavor to grasp matters entirely beyond its

range. Still, the teacher is wasting time; and, when
she ascertains that her pupils' previous repetitions of
things she wished them to say, mean nothing to them,
she may do harm by endeavoring to force them to
understand.

Lines of Work. Of course, oral problems are to occupy a fair portion of the time given to number work and even some
written problems should be given; but a large part of
the energy of the beginning pupils should be given to
abstract written addition and to the necessary oral
drills.   The following are the lines of work that
should be followed throughout the arithmetical course:
1st, oral problems, to develop proper ideas of number,
and to strengthen the reasoning powers; 2d, oral drills
in rapidly combining abstract numbers, to give the
necessary facility in performing written operations;
3d, written addition, subtraction, etc., of abstract
numbers; 4th, written solution of problems.

Oral Problems. The oral problems will be of two kinds: First,
those in which the child will have to determine for
himself the operation involved; and these should contain small numbers, so that the size of the numbers
will not make the problem unnecessarily difficult,
while failing to help the pupil's mathematical development.   In those of the second kind, which hardly
deserve to be called "problems," except that they are
"concrete," the chief object is to drill the pupil in
making the needed combination rapidly without a
pencil; they should involve, therefore, as a rule, but
one operation.

Drills. The oral drills should be given very frequently, but
for very short periods; and they should demand rapid
answers on the part of the pupils.   These help the

scholars in their subsequent abstract written work. Sight drills must not be overlooked.

The written problems show the pupils the applications of the fundamental processes to the ordinary affairs of life.

The ideal arithmetic should contain each of the **Careful** foregoing lines of work, carefully graded, and in the **Gradation** proper proportion. The book should be divided into sections, each containing the work of a year or a half year. The attempt to divide by daily lessons is unwise; as nobody but the teacher can determine just what subject requires special attention at a given time, with a corresponding number of examples.

The abstract work should be developed very slowly **Abstract** and carefully, with a very, very large number of ex- **Work,** amples. Difficulties should be encountered one at a time. As facility in calculation is obtained only by very much practice, it is almost impossible to furnish too many abstract examples. The task of selecting them from other arithmetics, or of making them, should not be thrown upon the over-burdened teacher; and it is better for the pupils to have them in their books than to be compelled to copy them from the blackboard. Reviews of processes already learned should be continued to the end of school life. The complaints of college professors and of business men that graduates of high schools cannot even add or multiply correctly is only too well founded.

As the chief object of the written problems is to **Written** develop reasoning power, they must, if possible, be **Problems.** even more carefully graded than the abstract work. A problem should generally require no explanation from the teacher; the conditions, therefore, should be

such as are reasonably familiar to the pupil.   This requires an author to skillfully adapt the wording of a
problem, and the matters contained in it, to the age of
the average pupil that will be required to work it.   The
numbers employed should not be so large as to daze
the learner; since the latter, as a rule, stumbles over a
written problem expressed in the same words and containing the same conditions as an oral one with smaller
figures that gives him no trouble whatever.   This latter difficulty can frequently be overcome by using
written problems as "sight" ones, the numbers being
changed by the pupil to those small enough to be handled without a pencil, and the pupil then working the
problem again with the figures given in the book.

"Miscellane-ous" Problems. Problems, both oral and written, should always be
"miscellaneous;" that is, there should be no heading
to indicate the character of the operation required to
solve one.   If the scholar knows that all the so-called
problems on a given page involve multiplication, he
need give no attention to the conditions.   No two
consecutive problems should involve the same operations, except in the few cases where two or more successive ones are introduced to lead up to a more complicated one.

While problems constitute a very important part of
a child's arithmetical training, progress in abstract
work should not be retarded by the teacher, in the
vain attempt to make each pupil work out and understand every problem.   The wise teacher will not require every member of the class to keep pace with his

Analysis of Problems. mates in problems, nor will she require all to work the
same problems at the same time, nor will she insist
upon any pupil solving all of them.   She will also in

problem work, both oral and written, assume that the child has reasoned correctly when he gets the correct answer; and, therefore, she will not exact an unmeaning analysis, oral or written. If she wishes the pupil to give a reason, she will take any one suited to the child's years, even if it does not contain the conventional "wherefore" or "hence." She will not expect written solutions to follow a set plan, nor will she spoil a bright boy by requiring him to place upon his paper any more figures than are necessary to aid him in obtaining the result. An occasional written analysis, as an exercise in composition, she will probably ask.

While the science of arithmetic has no place in the elementary school, and while the "how" should generally precede the "why," the thoughtful instructor will give her brighter pupils an opportunity to develop power by reasoning out the "how," before she shows it to the slower ones. After pupils have added numbers of two figures that need no "carrying," she might lead up to the latter, by asking on the board the sum of 12 and 12, then 13 and 13, then 14 and 14, then 15 and 15. Some members of her class would know that the sum of the last set is 30, even if the oral combinations had been confined to numbers of one figure; and they would appreciate the method that produces this result. Subtraction as the reverse of addition should be led up to; but no time should be spent in explaining the reason for the method employed. Those that can get any benefit from the perliminary work, should be permitted to get it; but as the "why" will come anyhow, although later, the progress of the class should not be delayed. The

Development of Power.

addition of 15 and 15 will show pupils how to get the product of 15 by 2, after they have worked multiplication examples in which there is no "carrying."

As the child grows older, and as his reasoning power increases, he should be given more frequent opportunities to develop for himself the so-called **Development of "Rules."** "rules." All that is necessary in the case of most children is that the teacher should furnish examples in which the successive steps occur in the proper order. She need scarcely say a word in explanation; in fact, the better the teacher the fewer her words, if she takes care to present difficulties no more rapidly than they can be surmounted.

Topical Work. The working-out of this kind of work is hardly possible in the old-time book. Each topic has to be contained in a chapter, of which the padding constitutes a large part. Work that is best spread over a year or so, and in which results are to be obtained only after working hundreds of examples, has to be dismissed in a few pages.

The erroneous notion formerly prevalent, that pupils were somehow improved by over-difficult tasks, prevented the adoption in this country of the use of **Arithmetic vs. Algebra.** algebraic methods by students of arithmetic. While the old-timer was ready to admit that some of the so-called arithmetic problems could be solved in a quarter of the time by the use of the letter x, he pretended to believe that it was a good thing for the child to make him attempt the almost impossible. Although Spartan methods of killing off the weaklings have long been discontinued on the physical side, the school life of many has been made unnecessarily severe by requiring them to attempt to solve problems in the hardest way, because of the supposed mental growth thereby induced. It signifies nothing to the believers in this plan that much the larger number of pupils get nothing out of it; they are content at the success of the fortunate few.

The opponents of the introduction of algebraic **Formal** methods into the elementary school claim that this **Study of Algebra.** subject should be confined exclusively to those able to go to a high school. While it may be true that the formal study of algebra as a science should not be commenced until about the ninth school year, no one will have the hardihood to assert that other pupils should be deprived of the use of anything that would tend to lighten their burdens.

Even the fiercest opponent of the use of x in a so-called arithmetical problem, will himself, in solving **Arithmetical** such a problem, make use of an algebraic method; **Circumlocu-** but to conceal the latter, he will explain his solution **tion.** by a tedious circumlocution in which the tale-telling x is carefully kept from view.

There is nothing in the application of algebraic **The use of x.** methods to the solution of problems that is beyond the capacity of the average child or teacher. If in a first-year class-room, you put on the blackboard $3+?=5$, the correct answer is given by nearly every pupil. While no one would object to such a problem as an arithmetical one, it is called algebra when an x is substituted for the interrogation point. Is this fair?

The mind of the average child works *forward*, so **Going** to speak, better than it works *backward*. A beginner **Forward.** in subtraction can tell the answer to "7 and what makes 10?" more readily than to "10 less 7 equals what?" The former is algebraic in a way; the latter, arithmetical.

The following problem, frequently found in the arithmetics, cannot be solved arithmetically without help, by any but the most phenomenal scholars of the age at which they reach it in the books: "The votes cast for A and B number 6836, of which A gets a majority of 748. How many does each receive?" An author (who has studied algebra) furnishes a neat explanation. His excuse for inserting this problem and many other similar ones is that children may meet them later in life. Instead of furnishing the general (algebraic) method, he gives a different, pretendedly arithmetical one for each, and the scholar can solve only those whose types he has already had, instead of being enabled by the algebraic master-key to open any lock, whether he has seen it before or not.

Problems in Interest. Let us see how the "problems" in interest are handled by arithmetic makers that are unwilling to give their clients the benefit of the simple methods. To find what principal will produce $64 in 3yr. 6mo. 9da. at 6%, they assume a principal of $1, on which the interest is calculated at the given rate for the given time. The result is found to be $0.2115. The pupil is then told that the required principal is as many times $1 as $64 is times $0.2115.

While the bright boy that had never seen algebra, could not of himself evolve the foregoing method, the bright student of algebra could solve the problem without having encountered it previously. Instead of finding the interest on $1 (which is almost as much algebra as arithmetic) he would calculate it on x dollars, and call this result—$.2115x$—equal to 64, the equation being, without decimals, $2115x = 640,000$. His practice in solving equations suggests the remaining step.

These interest problems are at least six in number:

1. Given interest, rate, time, to find principal.
2. Given principal, rate, interest, to find time.
3. Given principal, time, interest, to find rate.
4. Given amount, rate, time, to find principal.
5. Given amount, rate, principal, to find time.
6. Given amount, time, principal, to find rate.

While others might be enumerated, the foregoing are sufficient to show the advisability of applying algebraic methods when they are available. These six "problems" really should constitute no "problem" of special note from the algebraic standpoint. Anyone that knows a little of algebraic ways, and able to calculate interest, needs no "rule". He works out the interest (or amount), using x to represent the missing factor, and he then forms the necessary equation. By following the old way, the learner is required to memorize six rules; especially as the text-book maker fails to make clear the connection between them. Not knowing the underlying reasons, he forgets the rules shortly after leaving school, and he becomes helpless. The algebra boy gets no "rule" for solving any problem, except to treat the x just as he would the number it represents. *General Method vs. Special Method.*

As most teachers are from high or normal schools, or both, but very few will be compelled to make any special study of the algebraic method. These few, if competent to teach arithmetic, can make themselves familiar with the method after very little practice. *Easy to Learn.*

The writer of these lines deprecates the attempts of some misguided people who seek to introduce *formal* algebra into the grammar school course, reasoning that it will save time later in the high school. The *High school Algebra.*

elementary course is intended primarily for those whose education ends there. Nothing should be introduced that needs high school work to give it any value. A boy that gives a year or so to addition, subtraction, etc. of algebraic quantities gets no benefit whatever from the study, if he does not go to high school. This time should be given almost entirely to the solution of the equation. The pupils that go to the high school should begin the study of algebra at the beginning, just the same as those who had never seen it, except that they may progress much more rapidly from the insight given them of the utility of the new study. Diluted high school algebra should have no place in an eight years' course of study for the elementary schools. Those who propose it do not appreciate the real province of "algebra below the high school."

While a few French and German schools postpone algebra until a late period of the elementary school course, they all introduce geometry very early in the child's school life, the French schools beginning it during the first year.

Grammar school Geometry. As we do not teach high school algebra when we use x in the arithmetic work of the lower schools, the word "geometry" as employed in European courses of study does not mean that demonstrative geometry is inflicted **Constructive Work.** upon infants. Geometry is begun in France, as in the United States, by clay modeling, drawing squares and circles, constructing paper prisms and cones. It includes mensuration of surfaces and of solids, as well as the solution of simple problems in construction. It does not mean the study of the high school text-book.

For every pupil of the elementary school that will be called upon to work out an example in partial payments, there will be a thousand likely to require some knowledge of geometrical facts. These facts should be commenced in the lower school at as early an age as possible. The drawing courses in many schools, urban and rural, provide the best possible instruction for the smaller children. By the end of the fourth year systematic work should come into the arithmetic work, a little at a time. Mensuration of rectangles, formerly left for the end of the eighth year, and later pushed forward a year or so, should commence at the beginning of the fifth year. Each year of the last four should contain its proper share of calculating surfaces and volumes; and the last year or two should contain a well worked-out set of construction problems, the working of which would put the pupil in possession of the most important facts of geometry. *Utility of Geometry.*

As in algebra, the injudicious should not be permitted to push demonstrative geometry into elementary schools. The latter is studied in the high school for its disciplinary value. The constructive work of the other, besides being extremely valuable to those quitting school at the end of the eighth year, is also useful to the later student of Euclid or of Legendre. Knowing the facts, he is better able to appreciate the chain of reasoning employed in the text-book. *Demonstrative Geometry.*

It is hardly necessary to enumerate the persons to whom some knowledge of geometrical facts is useful. The farmer, mason, plasterer, carpenter, tinsmith, painter, have all to deal with mensuration to a greater or less extent, and also with the construction of some of the geometrical forms. *A Needed Study.*

The work in constructive geometry can be done by comparatively young children. What the latter *Easily Taught.*

can readily do, should present no difficulty to the teacher.

The question of time is always an important one in. the present over-crowded course. Friends (or enemies) of the schools are continually coming to the front with additional studies to be inflicted upon the system, and those teachers are hardly blamable who look with **How to Find Time.** disfavor upon the attempt to add algebra and geometry to the over-loaded curriculum. If, however, they realize that there is no desire to introduce the high-school subjects known by these names, that all that is intended is to suggest the employment of a few simple algebraic expedients in solving arithmetic problems, and the use of drawing as an aid in mensuration work, their objections will be less vigorous.

The benefits to teachers and scholars will be increased if the adoption of the new method leads to better arrangement of the old topics and the elimination of every unnecessary one. By cutting out the things **Cutting out Useless Topics.** that now overload the books, the time at present given to arithmetic may be lessened, the subject will be better taught, and plenty of time will be found to use the equation and to work out problems in construction.

III.

PLAN AND SCOPE OF THE WALSH BOOKS.

The Walsh arithmetics constitute a one-book series bound for convenience in two or in three parts. The first page of one book follows immediately after the last page of the preceding one, without a break. The purchaser of the second book does not buy a number of useless pages, as he must frequently do in the case of other series.

No Waste Matter.

Each arithmetic chapter after the first contains work for a half year. Besides the appropriate advance work in all the lines, oral and written, drill work and problems, it contains the necessary reviews.

Half-year Chapters.

Children will not willingly turn backward to get matter for reviews. The advisability of taking new lessons for this purpose is especially appreciated by teachers of language, English and ·foreign, ancient and modern. Besides, the need of constant review is likely to be overlooked unless matter for the purpose is brought directly to the teacher's attention.

Reviews.

Another strong feature is the careful grading. In the abstract work, the examples are so numerous that the difficulties are introduced as slowly as is compatible with good work. The very great number of the abstract examples gives the needed facility in rapid and accurate calculation. The examples are so graded that the child can begin written work early in his school life, and continue it without interruption. He can begin to add as soon as he knows a few sums, and

Large Number of Examples.

the successive examples grow difficult by slow degrees.
In the first nine pages, for instance, there are 258 examples in addition, oral and written, with the total of
each column less than 10. The children learn to do
by doing. Then follow 121 examples, problems, etc.,
leading to written subtraction, without "borrowing,'
then 65 examples in written subtraction and 10 "miscellaneous" problems, 454 examples in all before 10 is
used as a sum of any column or as a separate minuend.
In addition to the foregoing there are 93 exercises in
numeration and notation of numbers to 99, or 547 exercises of all kinds in the first fourteen pages. This
shows the absence of padding and the care taken in
the development of the work. The remaining 21
pages of the first chapter, devoted to addition and subtraction of easy numbers, contain 879 exercises of
all kinds, including drills, etc., making a total of 1426
for 35 pages. These will be none too many, as the
work of this chapter is intended to cover what is
usually done by the end of the second year.

The next chapter is arranged for pupils of the first
half of the third school year. It extends the previous
work in addition and subtraction, and takes up multiplication and division, beginning with the new work.
Multiplication is commenced at once on the supposi-
tion that the child has learned from his addition work
the products by 2 up to twice 4. Ten exercises and
60 examples are given with 2 as a multiplier, and
without carrying, to fasten the child's knowledge of
the early table. The last 10 examples introduce
larger products, but the examples still involve no carrying. Division by two is next taken up, with each
figure of the dividend a multiple of the divisor, the

**Multiplica-
tion and
Division.**

same number of exercises being employed as in multiplication.

After nearly a half dozen pages of review work and "miscellaneous" problems, also some extension of numeration and notation, pupils are led to "carrying" in multiplication by being asked to find products of 12, 13, 14, 15, 16 and 17 by 2. Then come the quotients of 24, 26, 28, 30, 34 and 38 divided by 2. It is left to the teacher to decide whether or not she needs to show the "how." When the pupil has used 2 as a multiplier and a divisor in a number of examples, he is plunged into a number of others in which the multipliers (or divisors) include numbers to 9. The work, however, is kept within his range by using in the multiplicand only (or quotient) numbers composed of 0's, 1's and 2's. From this he learns that he already knows a portion of the "3 times" table, also a portion of each of the others. *Development of Process by Pupils.* *Commutation.*

The child learns the "3 times" table by working numerous examples in multiplication and division with this number as the multiplier or the divisor. He then, as before, uses the other numbers to 9 as multipliers or divisors, with multiplicands or quotients limited to numbers made up of 0's, 1's, 2's and 3's. Working in this way, he not only learns each table easily and thoroughly, but he begins to understand the law of commutation, and to realize that as he goes towards 9 times, he has fewer facts to memorize in each table.

This lengthy explanation of the work of the first two chapters is intended to show how much attention has been paid to making the child's path in numbers as smooth and as interesting as possible. The shortness of the examples and the care to avoid introducing *Securing Child's Interest.*

difficulties too rapidly, tend to give the pupil a sense of power. This obtained, his interest is secured, and everything goes smoothly. When a child that has used only 2 as a multiplier is asked to multiply 121 by 3, 222 by 4, 201 by 5, 121 by 6, 202 by 7, 112 by 8, and 212 by 9, he is delighted to find that the new multipliers present no new difficulties, and he is encouraged in his onward course.

New Topics. In discussing the matter of the second chapter, no reference has been made to the drills, oral and sight, problems oral and written; nor to the new matters introduced—United States money, fractional parts of numbers, Roman notation, liquid measure. Each turn of the "spiral" brings in its new matter, besides amplifying and extending the old. It must not be supposed, either, that abstract work constitutes the sole important feature of the Walsh books.

Accuracy and Rapidity. These books lay as much stress on the reasoning side as do any other good books; but they also recognize the important fact that the ability to reason correctly in mathematics is useless if not accompanied by the ability to compute accurately. The early school years are the ones to be given to the endless examples needed to secure accuracy and rapidity in performing operations, as children at this period are ready and willing to give themselves up to the grind necessary to secure these results. If they haven't mastered the fundamental processes before they are 11 or 12, the chances are that they will always be slow and inaccurate.

Gradual Development. The care shown in the gradual development of the work contained in the first and second chapters extends to all the others. In long division, for instance, Chap-

ter IV, none of the first 300 examples has a dividend
of over four figures, although the multiplication results in the same chapter generally contain five figures.
As long division is rather difficult, the likelihood of
the pupil becoming discouraged is diminished by the
shortness of the examples, especially as the earlier
quotients consist of numbers containing small figures;
such as, 13, 21, 22, 23, 12, 211, 123, 222, 11, 12, etc.
The divisors, too, are carefully chosen; 21, 31, 41, 22,
32, 42, etc., being used before 16. The limit of four
figures in the dividends of the early examples permits
of the early introduction of large divisors without really increasing the difficulty of the example, since the
longer the divisor the fewer figures there will be in the
quotient; the answers to $8199 \div 911$ and $9872 \div 2468$
consisting of a single figure. A word will be said later
about the long-division drills.

A form of fraction work is begun very early. As **Fractions.**
soon as children learn to divide by 2, they find one-
half of a number. Later, they find fourths and thirds,
without, however, hearing of "fraction," "numerator," "denominator," or the like. The sum of $\frac{1}{2}$ and
$\frac{1}{2}$, and of $1\frac{1}{2}$ and $1\frac{1}{2}$, etc., begins addition of fractions in Chapter III, although the formal work is not
reached until Chapter VII. Each turn of the "spiral"
brings in its appropriate work in Chapters IV, V, and
VI, while each chapter after the seventh has the needed reviews.

Chapter II marks the commencement of work in **Denominate**
denominate numbers, with problems involving pints **Numbers.**
and quarts. The intervening chapters to the ninth
extend the child's knowledge of this important topic,
while the ninth summarizes and completes the subject,

except for the subsequent inevitable reviews. Long, tedious examples are avoided by limiting the number of denominate units in any example to two successive units before the ninth chapter, and to three successive units in the ninth and remaining chapters. This feature of short examples is a prominent one in the Walsh books, and it appeals to every one interested in education. The old time teacher that covered the blackboard with a single example in addition, for instance, did much to kill the pupils' interest in mathematics. A child that is given ten or a dozen short examples during an arithmetic lesson has a chance of getting the correct answer to a large proportion of them, while unable to continue the strain needed to work out a single very long one.

Short Examples.

From the beginning of the sixth chapter, the point at which pupils generally take up a second book, the superiority of the "spiral" method becomes more apparent. In the lower grades, many teachers do good work because they are not hampered by "logical" books in the pupils' hands. When the children of the 5th year get a book of this kind, they are fettered. The early pages, devoted to the fundamental processes, appear too elementary, and are not touched; while the topical arrangement prevents the extension, until it is regularly reached, of some work already begun. In the first chapter of the second Walsh book (Chapter VI) all the previous work is continued and extended, while new ground is broken in decimals and mensuration, each treated in such a way as to be readily understood by the 5th year scholar. A year later, Chapter VIII, marks the point at which are introduced percentage and interest.

The Old-time Book II.

The employment of the "spiral" method does not prevent the author of the Walsh books from adopting the good features of other books. The early introduction of an advanced topic is always accompanied by its systematic treatment in the chapter especially devoted to that topic, which chapter is reached in the Walsh books at just the same time it is reached in the old-line texts. Thus, Chapter VII of Walsh is the fraction one; Chapter VIII, the decimal one; Chapter IX, the denominate number one; Chapter XI, the next arithmetical one, being given to percentage; etc., etc.

Systematic Treatment of Topics.

Besides being strong in its general features, the Walsh books are particularly useful for teaching purposes because of their special features. One marked characteristic is the space devoted to "drills," oral and sight, each chapter containing its share. One kind of drills is intended to make children masters of all the combinations needed in their work in the fundamental processes, including two sets, never before used in this country, to enable pupils to obtain rapidly each figure of the quotient in a long division example. (See Art. 321 and Arts. 397—401.) These preliminary drills are furnished in great variety, to prevent the weariness to children that comes from tiresome repetitions of the same exercise.

Special Features.

As children brought up on the old books advanced into more advanced topics, they seemed to lose their earlier facility in computation, because of lack of reviews, discontinuance of drills, etc. The Walsh books aim not only to keep up the skill obtained in the lower classes in adding, multiplying, etc., mentally and on paper, but to increase it as far as possible. A business man should not need to hunt up a pencil every time he wishes to make a simple calculation. To enable a boy or a girl to readily combine large numbers, each half-yearly chapter has a page (or more) devoted to "special drills," which gradually increase in difficulty, as will be seen from an examination of the following selections:

Special Drills.

FROM CHAPTER III.

50+30	20+60	50+40	40+50	30+60
90—50	50—20	80—40	50—30	90—70
20×2	3×30	20×4	⅓×90	20×3
40÷2	90÷30	⅓ of 60	80÷4	40÷2

FROM CHAPTER IV.

13+13	19+30	43+46	51+37	22+23
25—13	31—20	65—11	87—75	46—26
13×2	32×3	21×4	23×3	41×2
88÷4	39÷13	26÷2	63÷21	86÷2

FROM CHAPTER V.

56+17	13+78	25+16	18+45	34+19
66—19	56—39	60—12	76—57	43—18
13×4	5×15	28×3	7×13	47×2
42÷3	42÷14	78÷6 `	78÷13	90÷6

The foregoing types indicate the gradual development of the drills; the next set, from Chapter XIV, shows what pupils of the eighth school year should be able to do without using a pencil:

112+91+85	43+131+61	95+144+79
150—23+48	172+ 19—66	183—(72—37)
63×28	54×42	26×58
676÷13	527÷17	704÷22
84×1⅛	211¼×13	36×49⅝

$$68+56+174$$
$$161+79-12$$
$$71\times82$$
$$837\div27$$
$$17\tfrac{3}{4}\div5\tfrac{1}{4}$$

After each set of drills, there are given many oral (or sight) problems involving similar combinations, a feature found in no other arithmetic, written or mental. The advanced mental examples, even in books devoted exclusively to this form of arithmetic, use smaller numbers as the work progresses, the authors considering, apparently, that facility in computation is of no value as compared with the ability to crack mathematic chestnuts. While the mental arithmetic work in the Walsh books includes examples and problems such as are described above, at the beginning of this paragraph, it also includes the customary exercises bearing upon the topic under immediate treatment.

Problems Involving the "Special Drills."

Other sets of drills have for their object the development of skill in the use of short methods by pupils. They include mental multiplication and division by fractional parts of 100; the use of 99, 24, 49, also of 99½, 24½, 49½, etc., as multipliers in mental examples, etc. The problems under this head, and, in fact, problems all through the books, show, where possible, the law of "commutation": for instance, that 25 yards at 48c. per yard can be solved mentally in the same way as 48 yards at 25c.; that in subtraction examples the child can take 43 from 50 when he can take 7 from 50; that, in multiplication, he knows 9 fours when he has learned 4 nines; that, in division, if 35 contains 5 sevens, it contains 7 fives.

Commutation Drills.

"Approxima-tion" Drills. The "approximation" drills are new to text books in arithmetic. Their value is appreciated on sight by all teachers anxious to prevent their pupils from offering absurd answers. The use of the method of approximation before attempting to solve a problem, will frequently lead a pupil to discover the operations necessary to its solution, whereas, the too frequent practice among average children is to begin to work without a full appreciation of the conditions involved.

With the purpose of making the arithmetical journey as smooth as possible for young learners, the Walsh arithmetics suggest some improvements upon the method now in vogue. Teachers that believe children should not do anything without a knowledge of the **New Method.** underlying reasons, have made subtraction unnecessarily difficult by requiring pupils to work examples in the "logical" way. In finding the difference between 835 and 398, the little learner is supposed to make a speech in some such fashion as this: "Eight units from 5 units I cannot take, so I borrow 1 ten from the 3 tens. Adding this ten, which equals 10 units, to the 5 units, I have 15 units. Then I take 8 units from 15 units which leaves me 7 units, and this I write in the units column. Since I took 1 ten from the 3 tens, I have two tens remaining. As I cannot take 9 tens from 2 tens I must borrow 1 hundred from the 8 hundreds. Adding this hundred, which equals ten tens," etc., etc.; but why continue this rigamarole? And how the difficulty is increased when the minuend contains a few ciphers, say 1000—473, where the "next higher order" has nothing to lend. The old way is just as "logical": 8 from 15 leaves 7, 10 from 13 leaves 3, 4 from 8 leaves 4; but it is more difficult

·to "explain". Is there, however, any likelihood that infants understand the explanation they profess to give of the other method? Should school children be required to repeat an unmeaning formula they will never use after leaving school? An accountant does not think of units, tens, or hundreds as he makes his daily calculations.

In the Walsh book, the "building up" method is advised; or, as it is sometimes called, the "computer's method." Instead of being told to take 8 from 15, the child is asked "8 and what make 15?" as experience shows that the mind travels forward more easily than it goes backward, especially after giving all its attention previously to addition. By this method the operation resembles addition so much as to make it less difficult for beginners. The use of this method enables the pupil to shorten many other operations. He can, for instance, ascertain the result of the following: $1000-(643+287+25)$ without first finding the sum of these numbers to be added, (Art. 384); or $4832-(456\times8)$. Long division can be performed without writing the partial products (Art. 616); or the mixed number equivalent to $\dfrac{11223}{1984}$ can be written at once.

Building-up Method in Subtraction.

In long division, the children are advised to write each quotient figure *above* the corresponding figure of the dividend, to prevent the omission of one or more ciphers in the quotient, or the introduction in the quotient of a figure too many (Art. 282). This plan is similar to the one used in short division; and it makes the necessary multiplication more easy to the young student by bringing the multiplying quotient figure nearer to the divisor—an important trifle.

Overhead Quotient.

Division of Decimals. The method given for "pointing-off" in division of decimals (Art. 663) is a mechanical one, but it prevents the pupil from getting the decimal point in the wrong place. Another good method, which helps by mechanical means in getting the correct answer in multiplication, is given in Art. 344. The intelligent teacher will not despise anything that will aid her pupils to secure accurate results, even if it is sneered at as "mechanical" by the user of "logical" methods whose pupils frequently blunder.

Short Method. . Besides giving much attention to special short methods, the Walsh books offer suggestions in every chapter as to the disuse of unnecessary figures. Children learn just as readily to cipher without these aids (?) as with them, and their written work becomes more accurate by not being too long drawn out. For instance, in finding the least common multiple of 3, 9, 7, 14, 6, 14, 2, 12, some teachers permit pupils to retain all these numbers, instead of using only the necessary ones—9, 14, 12 (Art. 595). In reducing 28⅞ to an improper fraction or in multiplying 16⅝ by 8, scholars are not required, as they should be, to write the answer directly (Art. 653).

To reduce 15 gal. 3 qt. to quarts, the average boy or girl will use several lines of figures, when one is sufficient (Art. 766); see also under interest (Art. 936), discount (Art. 937), commercial discount (Art. 944), **Omission of Unnecessary Figures.** compound interest (Art. 983). To enumerate all the places in which suggestions are made as to omitting unneccessary figures, would be to make too long a list. The index to the Grammar School Arithmetic gives 56 pages on which are found "short methods," and these do not include suggestions given in the Teachers' Manual.

The non-progressive teacher hesitates to do things in a strange way; but she will soon realize the advisability of saving time as indicated in the Walsh books. The methods given are the straightforward ones that can be understood by the dullest pupil, and which, by being applicable in the daily work, are readily appreciated. They do not include such as $9\frac{1}{2} \times 9\frac{1}{2}$, 85×85, 64×66, found in some old magazine under the head of "Mathematical Recreations."

The algebra work is contained in chapters X and XV; of these, every pupil should study the former. It contains only 11 pages, and is readily understood **Algebra.** by a very young pupil. To enable a teacher unfamiliar with this work to do it successfully, she has only to follow the lines laid down in the Manual. While chapter XV is intended more particularly for schools that have a nine-years' course, its study is advised even if time has to be obtained therefor by the omission of some of the work in arithmetic: bonds and stocks, for instance, compound interest, exchange, partial payments, proportion, equation of payments, etc.

While the construction exercises and problems have been placed in chapter XVI, they should be commenced about the time chapter XII is reached, and carried along with the arithmetic work, even if portions of the latter receive less attention in consequence. The exercises in calculating heights and distances are very in- **Geometry.** teresting to scholars and are very useful to many of them later in life. They are likely to be employed by more pupils than the problems in equation of payments.

The teacher will find in the Manual minute directions as to the best way to conduct the geometry lessons.

The Walsh books furnish problems in greater number and variety than any other series. Each problem, being unlike the previous one, will require the pupil to read it carefully; he cannot work it by referring to a "sample" one at the head of the page. The absurd types are all omitted, such as the far-fetched ones in some books under the headings of greatest common divisor and least common multiple.

These books are offered to the teaching profession in the belief that they contain more strong features and are better teaching books than any now before the public. It is not, however, claimed that they are perfect as books of reference. Although an index is really unnecessary in a teaching book, a good one is furnished for such teachers as desire to use the book topically.

The Walsh Arithmetics

Contain abundant, varied, and practical problems.
Omit nothing essential, yet contain only the essentials.
Are fresh, original, and well graded.
Secure constant review without actual repetition.
Are arranged on the "spiral" plan.

. Three=Book Series.

Elementary Arithmetic.— For third and fourth grades.

Cloth. 218 pages. 30 cents

Intermediate Arithmetic.— For fifth and sixth grades.

Cloth. 252 pages. 35 cents.

Higher Arithmetic.— For upper grades.

Half Leather. 387 pages. 65 cents.

Two-Book Series.

Primary Arithmetic.— For third, fourth and fifth grades.

Cloth. 198 pages. 30 cents.

Grammar School Arithmetic.— For upper grades.

Half Leather. 433 pages. 65 cents.

Each series is provided with Teacher's Manuals in parts.
Correspondence is cordially invited.

D. C. HEATH & CO., Publishers, Boston, New York, Chicago.

Mathematics for Common Schools.

A graded course in arithmetic, with simple problems in algebra and geometry. By JOHN H. WALSH, Associate Superintendent of Public Instruction, Brooklyn. **Two-Book Series.** — *Primary Arithmetic.* Cloth, 206 pages. Introduction price, 30 cents. *Grammar School Arithmetic.* Half leather, 458 pages. Introduction price, 65 cents.

Three-Book Series. — *Elementary Arithmetic.* Cloth, 220 pages. Introduction price, 30 cents. *Intermediate Arithmetic.* Cloth, 255 pages. Introduction price, 35 cents. *Higher Arithmetic.* Half leather, 403 pages. Introduction price, 65 cents.

IN several important particulars the Walsh Arithmetics mark a departure from the traditional method and arrangement.

1. By the "spiral advancement plan" the *elements* of all the important topics are taken up early in the course, adding to the interest and practical worth of the study.

2. In each case the subject taken up is not exhausted at once, but practice in it is carried on with problems of gradually increasing difficulty throughout the course.

3. Drills in addition, subtraction, multiplication and division of abstract numbers are given at intervals throughout the books of the series, thus insuring in pupils of the upper grades, accuracy and speed in the fundamental processes. This is an important and unique feature.

4. The series contains a larger number of varied and practical *concrete* problems than any other.

5. It is the only series containing drills in securing "approximate answers," — work of great advantage in calling the pupil's attention to the condition of a problem, and thus giving the power to detect at once the absurdity of any result greatly wide of the mark.

Such obvious merits of the lower books as the alternation of oral, sight and written work, the early introduction of United States currency (leading to decimals), the easy beginnings with fractions and denominate numbers, and the freshness and interest insured by the great variety of means used to secure perfect mastery of simple number combinations, cannot be too strongly emphasized.

In the higher book are to be noted the wide range of subjects treated in their simple elements, the great variety of practical problems, the early introduction of percentage and simple interest, of bills and receipts, and all the matters connected with simple commercial arithmetic.

Unique features are : the many short methods noted, the use of approximate answers, the abundant drills in the four fundamental processes, and the introduction of algebra in a way so natural and simple that children of ten may easily grasp enough of it to shorten many of the longer arithmetical processes.

The Walsh Arithmetics constitute a one-book series bound for convenience in two or in three parts. The first page of one book follows immediately after the last page of the preceding one, without a break. The purchaser of the second book does not buy a number of useless pages, as he must frequently do in the case of other series.

The Walsh books illustrate most admirably what every teacher knows so well, that many things that are complex in their completeness, are in their elements simply and easily comprehended by young children.

The series thoroughly satisfies demands of modern pedagogy ; it is inductive in method, practical and varied in treatment, makes clear thought and accurate computation matters of habit, and lays the foundation for the intelligent use of mathematical principles.

The Walsh Arithmetics anticipated the recommendations of the Committee of Ten and of the Committee of Fifteen.

Full descriptive circular, and valuable pamphlets upon "The Spiral Method" and "Suggestions to Teachers and Courses of Study in Arithmetic" sent free on request.

Teachers' Manuals to *Mathematics for Common Schools.*

By JOHN H. WALSH, Associate Sup't of Public Instruction, Brooklyn, N. Y.

Manual to Three-Book edition. Complete. 385 pages. Cloth. Retail price, $1.50.
Manual to Elementary Arithmetic. 63 pages. Paper. Retail price, 15 cents.
Manual to Intermediate Arithmetic. 124 pages. Paper. Retail price, 20 cents.
Manual to Higher Arithmetic. 343 pages. Paper. Retail price, 40 cents.
Manual to Primary Arithmetic. 67 pages. Paper. Retail price, 15 cents.
Manual to Grammar School Arithmetic. 342 pages. Paper. Retail price, 50 cents.

Elementary Mathematics

Atwood's Complete Graded Arithmetic. Presents a carefully graded course, to begin with the fourth year and continue through the eighth year. Part I, 30 cts.; Part II, 65 cts.

Badlam's Aids to Number. Teacher's edition — First series, Nos. 1 to 10, 40 cts.; Second series, Nos. 10 to 20, 40 cts. Pupil's edition — First series, 25 cts.; Second series, 25 cts.

Branson's Methods in Teaching Arithmetic. 15 cts.

Hanus's Geometry in the Grammar Schools. An essay, with outline of work for the last three years of the grammar school. 25 cts.

Howland's Drill Cards. For middle grades in arithmetic. Each, 3 cts.; per hundred, $2.40.

Hunt's Geometry for Grammar Schools. The definitions and elementary concepts are to be taught concretely, by much measuring, and by the making of models and diagrams by the pupils. 30 cts.

Pierce's Review Number Cards. Two cards, for second and third year pupils. Each, 3 cts.; per hundred, $2.40.

Safford's Mathematical Teaching. A monograph, with applications. 25 cts.

Sloane's Practical Lessons in Fractions. 25 cts. Set of six fraction cards, for pupils to cut. 10 cts.

Sutton and Kimbrough's Pupils' Series of Arithmetics. Lower Book, for primary and intermediate grades, 35 cts. Higher Book, 65 cts.

The New Arithmetic. By 300 teachers. Little theory and much practice. An excellent review book. 65 cts.

Walsh's Arithmetics. On the "spiral advancement" plan, and perfectly graded. Special features of this series are its division into half-yearly chapters instead of the arrangement by topics; the great number and variety of the problems; the use of the equation in solution of arithmetical problems; and the introduction of the elements of algebra and geometry. Its use shortens and enriches the course in common school mathematics. In two series: —

Three Book Series — Elementary, 30 cts.; Intermediate, 35 cts.; Higher, 65 cts.
Two Book Series — Primary, 30 cts.; Grammar school, 65 cts.

Walsh's Algebra and Geometry for Grammar Grades. Three chapters from Walsh's Arithmetic printed separately. 15 cts.

White's Two Years with Numbers. For second and third year classes. 35 cts.

White's Junior Arithmetic. For fourth and fifth years. 45 cts.

White's Senior Arithmetic. 65 cts.

For advanced works see our list of books in Mathematics.

D. C. HEATH & CO., Publishers, Boston, New York, Chicago

THE WALSH ARITHMETICS

SUGGESTIONS TO TEACHERS

AND

OUTLINES OF COURSES OF STUDY

THREE-BOOK SERIES { Elementary Arithmetic . . . Introduction price, 30 cents
Intermediate Arithmetic . . "   " 35 "
Higher Arithmetic . . . . . "   " 65 "

TWO-BOOK SERIES { Primary Arithmetic. . . . . Introduction price, 30 cents
Grammar School Arithmetic, "   " 65 "

D. C. HEATH & CO., PUBLISHERS

BOSTON   NEW YORK   CHICAGO   LONDON

CONTENTS. — PART I.

———◦○◦———

CHAPTER I.

CHAPTER II.

v

CHAPTER III.

CHAPTER IV.

CONTENTS. — PART II.

—◆◆◆—

CHAPTER VI.

CHAPTER VII.

CHAPTER VIII.

CHAPTER IX.

CHAPTER X.

CONTENTS. — PART III.

CHAPTER XI.

CHAPTER XII.

CHAPTER XIII.

CHAPTER XIV.

CHAPTER XV.

CHAPTER XVI.

SUGGESTIONS TO TEACHERS

INTRODUCTORY

Plan and Scope of the Work. — In addition to the subjects generally included in text-books in arithmetic, *The Walsh Arithmetics* contain such simple work in algebraic equations and constructive geometry as can be studied to advantage by pupils of the elementary schools. The arithmetical portion is divided into thirteen chapters, each of which, except the first, contains a half-year's work. The following nine-year and eight-year courses will show the arrangement of topics :

NINE-YEAR COURSE

FIRST AND SECOND YEARS

Chapter I. — Numbers of Three Figures. Simple Processes.

THIRD YEAR

Chapters II. and III. — Numbers of Five Figures. Multipliers and Divisors of One Figure. Addition and Subtraction of Halves, of Fourths, of Thirds. Multiplication by Mixed Numbers. Pint, Quart, and Gallon ; Ounce and Pound. Roman Notation.

FOURTH YEAR

Chapters IV. and V. — Numbers of Six Figures. Multipliers and Divisors of Two or More Figures. Addition and Subtraction of Easy Fractions. Multiplication by Mixed Numbers. Simple Denominate Numbers. Roman Notation.

FIFTH YEAR

Chapters VI. and VII. — Fractions. Decimals of Three Places. Bills. Denominate Numbers. Simple Measurements.

SIXTH YEAR

Chapters VIII. and IX. — Decimals. Bills. Denominate Numbers. Surfaces and Volumes. Percentage and Interest.

1

Seventh Year

Chapters X. and XI. and Articles 931 to 963 in Chapter XII., and Articles 1251 to 1269 in Chapter XVI. — Percentage. Measurements. Interest. Discount. Surfaces and Volumes. Elementary Algebra and Geometry. Exercises and Problems.

Eighth Year

Chapter XII., Articles 964 to 1007, Chapter XIII., and Article 1270 of Chapter XVI. — Partnership. Bonds and Stocks. Compound Interest. Exchange. Longitude and Time. Partial Payments. Surfaces and Volumes. Square Root. Ratio. Proportion. Measurements. Elementary Geometry. Problems in Construction.

Ninth Year

Chapters XIV. and XV., and Chapter XVI. completed. — Equation of Payments. Mensuration of Plane Surfaces and Volumes. Cube Root. Annual Interest. Metric System. Elementary Algebra. Elementary Geometry. Calculation of Heights and Distances.

EIGHT-YEAR COURSE

First, Second, Third, and Fourth Years

As in nine-year course.

Fifth Year

Chapters VI. and VII. — Fractions. Decimals of Three Places. Bills. Denominate Numbers. Simple Measurements.

Sixth Year

Chapters VIII. and IX. — Decimals. Bills. Denominate Numbers. Surfaces and Volumes. Percentage and Interest.

Seventh Year

Chapters XI. and XII. — Percentage and Interest. Commercial and Bank Discount. Cause and Effect. Partnership. Bonds and Stocks. Exchange. Longitude and Time. Surfaces and Volumes.

Eighth Year

Chapters XIII. and XIV. — Partial Payments. Equation of Payments. Annual Interest. Metric System. Evolution and Involution. Surfaces and Volumes.

While all of the above topics are generally included in an eight years' course, it may be considered advisable to omit some of them, and to take up, instead, during the seventh and eighth years, the constructive geometry work of Chapter XVI. Among the topics that may be dropped without injury to the pupil are Bonds and Stocks, Exchange, Partial Payments, and Equation of Payments.

Grammar School Algebra. — Chapter X., consisting of a dozen pages, is devoted to the subject of easy equations of one unknown quantity, as a preliminary to the employment of the equation in so much of the subsequent work in arithmetic as is rendered more simple by this mode of treatment. To teachers desirous of dispensing with rules, sample solutions of type examples, etc., the algebraic method of solving the so-called " problems " in percentage, interest, discount, etc., is strongly recommended.

In Chapter XV., intended chiefly for schools having a nine years' course, the algebraic work is extended to cover simple equations containing two or more unknown quantities, and pure and affected quadratic equations of one unknown quantity.

No attempt has been made in these two chapters to treat algebra as a science; the aim has been to make grammar-school pupils acquainted, to some slight extent, with the great instrument of mathematical investigation, — the equation.

Constructive Geometry. — Progressive teachers will appreciate the importance of supplementing the concrete geometrical instruction now given in the drawing and mensuration work. Chapter XVI. contains a series of problems in construction so arranged as to enable pupils to obtain for themselves a working knowledge of all the most important facts of geometry. Applications of the facts thus ascertained, are made to the mensuration of surfaces and volumes, the calculation of heights and distances, etc. No attempt is made to anticipate the work of the high-school by teaching geometry as a science.

While the construction problems are brought together into a single chapter at the end of the book, it is not intended that instruction in geometry should be delayed until the preceding work is completed. Chapter XVI. should be commenced not later than the seventh year, and should be continued throughout the remainder of the grammar-school course. For the earlier years, suitable exercises in the mensuration of the surfaces of triangles and quadrilaterals, and of the volumes of right parallelopipedons have been incorporated with the arithmetic work.

II

GENERAL HINTS

Division of the Work. — The five chapters constituting Part I. of *Mathematics for Common Schools* should be completed by the end of the fourth school year. The remaining eight arithmetic chapters constitute half-yearly divisions for the second four years of school. Chapter I., with the additional oral work needed in the case of young pupils, will occupy about two years; the remaining four chapters should not take more than half a year each. When the Grube system is used, and the work of the first two years is exclusively oral, it will be possible, by omitting much of the easier portions of the first two chapters, to cover, during the third year, the ground contained in Chapters I., II., and III.

Additions and Omissions. — The teacher should freely supplement the work of the text-book when she finds it necessary to do so; and she should not hesitate to leave a topic that her pupils fully understand, even though they may not have worked all the examples given in connection therewith. A very large number of exercises is necessary for such pupils as can devote a half-year to the study of the matter furnished in each chapter. In the case of pupils of greater maturity, it will be possible to make more rapid progress by passing to the next topic as soon as the previous work is fairly well understood.

Oral and Written Work. — The heading "Slate Problems" is merely a general direction, and it should be disregarded by the teacher when the pupils are able to do the work "mentally." The use of the pencil should be demanded only so far as it may

5

be required. It is a pedagogical mistake to insist that all of the pupils of a class should set down a number of figures that are not needed by the brighter ones. As an occasional exercise, it may be advisable to have scholars give all the work required to solve a problem, and to make a written explanation of each step in the solution; but it should be the teacher's aim to have the majority of the examples done with as great rapidity as is consistent with absolute correctness. It will be found that, as a rule, the quickest workers are the most accurate.

Many of the slate problems can be treated by some classes as "sight" examples, each pupil reading the question for himself from the book, and writing the answer at a given signal without putting down any of the work.

Use of Books. — It is generally recommended that books be placed in pupils' hands as early as the third school year. Since many children are unable at this stage to read with sufficient intelligence to understand the terms of a problem, this work should be done under the teacher's direction, the latter reading the questions while the pupils follow from their books. In later years, the problems should be solved by the pupils from the books with practically no assistance whatever from the teacher.

Conduct of the Recitation. — Many thoughtful educators consider it advisable to divide an arithmetic class into two sections, for some purposes, even where its members are nearly equal in attainments. The members of one division of such a class may work examples from their books while the others write the answers to oral problems given by the teacher, etc.

Where a class is thus taught in two divisions, the members of each should sit in alternate rows, extending from the front of the room to the rear. Seated in this way, a pupil is doing a different kind of work from those on the right and the left, and he would not have the temptation of a neighbor's slate to lead him to compare answers.

As an economy of time, explanations of new subjects might be given to the whole class; but much of the arithmetic work should be done in "sections," one of which is under the immediate direction of the teacher, the other being employed in "seat" work. In the case of pupils of the more advanced classes, "seat" work should consist largely of "problems" solved without assistance. Especial pains have been taken to so grade the problems as to have none beyond the capacity of the average pupil that is willing to try to understand its terms. It is not necessary that all the members of a division should work the same problems at a given time, nor the same number of problems, nor that a new topic should be postponed until all of the previous problems have been solved.

Whenever it is possible, all of the members of the division working under the teacher's immediate direction should take part in all the work done. In mental arithmetic, for instance, while only a few may be called upon for explanations, all of the pupils should write the answers to each question. The same is true of much of the sight work, the approximations, some of the special drills, etc.

Drills and Sight Work. — To secure reasonable rapidity, it is necessary to have regular systematic drills. They should be employed daily, if possible, in the earlier years, but should never last longer than five or ten minutes. Various kinds are suggested, such as sight addition drills, in Arts. 3, 11, 24, 26, etc.; subtraction, in Arts. 19, 50, 53, etc.; multiplication, in Arts. 71, 109, etc.; division, in Arts. 199, 202, etc.; counting by 2's, 3's, etc., in Art. 61; carrying, in Art. 53, etc. For the young pupil, those are the most valuable in which the figures are in his sight, and in the position they occupy in an example; see Arts. 3, 34, 164, etc.

Many teachers prepare cards, each of which contains one of the combinations taught in their respective grades. Showing one of these cards, the teacher requires an immediate answer from a pupil. If his reply is correct, a new card is shown to the next pupil, and so on. Other teachers write a number of combinations on the blackboard, and point to them at random, requiring prompt answers. When drills remain on the board for any considerable time, some children learn to know the results of a combination by its location on the board, so that frequent changes in the arrangement of the drills are, therefore, advisable. The drills in Arts. 111, 112, and 115 furnish a great deal of work with the occasional change of a single figure.

For the higher classes, each chapter contains appropriate drills, which are subsequently used in oral problems. It happens only too frequently that as children go forward in school they lose much of the readiness in oral and written work they possessed in the lower grades, owing to the neglect of their teachers to continue to require quick, accurate review work in the operations previously taught. These special drills follow the plan of the combinations of the earlier chapters, but gradually grow more difficult. They should first be used as sight exercises, either from the books or from the blackboard.

To secure valuable results from drill exercises, the utmost possible promptness in answers should be insisted upon.

Definitions, Principles, and Rules. — Young children should not memorize rules or definitions. They should learn to add by adding, after being first shown by the teacher how to perform the operation. Those not previously taught by the Grube method should be given no reason for "carrying." In teaching such children to write numbers of two or three figures, there is nothing gained by discussing the local value of the digits. During the earlier years, instruction in the art of arithmetic should be given with the least possible amount of science. While principles may be incidentally brought to the view of the children at times, there should be no cross-examination thereon. It may be shown, for instance, that subtraction is the reverse of addition, and that multiplication is a short method of combining equal numbers, etc.; but care should be taken in the case of pupils below about the fifth school year not to dwell long on this side of the instruction. By that time, pupils should be able to add, subtract, multiply, and divide whole numbers; to add and subtract simple mixed numbers, and to use a mixed number as a multiplier or a multiplicand; to solve easy problems, with small numbers, involving the foregoing operations and others containing the more commonly used denominate units. Whether or not they can explain the principles underlying the operations is of next to no importance, if they can do the work with reasonable accuracy and rapidity.

When decimal fractions are taken up, the principles of Arabic notation should be developed; and about the same time, or somewhat later, the principles upon which are founded the operations in the fundamental processes, can be briefly discussed.

Definitions should in all cases be made by the pupils, their mistakes being brought out by the teacher through appropriate questions, criticisms, etc. Systematic work under this head should be deferred until at least the seventh year.

The use of unnecessary rules in the higher grades is to be deprecated. When, for instance, a pupil understands that *per cent* means *hundredths*, that seven per cent means seven hundredths, it should not be necessary to tell him that 7 per cent of 143 is obtained by multiplying 143 by .07. It should be a fair assumption that his previous work in the multiplication of common and of decimal fractions has enabled him to see that 7 per cent of 143 is $\frac{7}{100}$ of 143 or 143 × .07, without information other than the meaning of the term " per cent."

When a pupil is able to calculate that 15 % of 120 is 18, he should be allowed to try to work out for himself, without a rule, the solution of this problem: 18 is what per cent of 120? or of this: 18 is 15 % of what number? These questions should present no more difficulty in the seventh year than the following examples in the fifth: (*a*) Find the cost of $\frac{3}{20}$ ton of hay at $12 per ton. (*b*) When hay is worth $12 per ton, what part of a ton can be bought for $1.80? (c) If $\frac{3}{20}$ ton of hay costs $1.80, what is the value of a ton?

When, however, it becomes necessary to assist pupils in the solution of problems of this class, it is more profitable to furnish them with a general method by the use of the equation, than with any special plan suited only to the type under immediate discussion.

In the supplement to the Manual will be found the usual definitions, principles, and rules, for the teacher to use in such a way as her experience shows to be best for her pupils. The rules given are based somewhat on the older methods, rather than on those recommended by the author. He would prefer to omit entirely those relating to percentage, interest, and the like as being unnecessary, but that they are called for by many successful teachers, who prefer to continue the use of methods which they have found to produce satisfactory results.

Language. — While the use of correct language should be insisted upon in all lessons, children should not be required in arithmetic to give all answers in "complete sentences." Especially in the drills, it is important that the results be expressed in the fewest possible words.

Analyses. — Sparing use of analyses is recommended for beginners. If a pupil solves a problem correctly, the natural inference should be that his method is correct, even if he be unable to state it in words. When a pupil gives the analysis of a problem, he should be permitted to express himself in his own way. Set forms should not be used under any circumstances.

Objective Illustrations. — The chief reason for the use of objects in the study of arithmetic is to enable pupils to work without them. While counters, weights and measures, diagrams, or the like are necessary at the beginning of some topics, it is important to discontinue their use as soon as the scholar is able to proceed without their aid.

Approximate Answers. — An important drill is furnished in the "approximations." (See Arts. 521, 669, 719, etc.) Pupils should be required in much of their written work to estimate the result before beginning to solve a problem with the pencil. Besides preventing an absurd answer, this practice will also have the effect of causing a pupil to see what processes are necessary. In too many instances, work is commenced upon a problem before the conditions are grasped by the youthful scholar; which will be less likely to occur in the case of one who has carefully "estimated" the answer. The pupil will frequently find, also, that he can obtain the correct result without using his pencil at all.

Indicating Operations. — It is a good practice to require pupils to indicate by signs all of the processes necessary to the solution of a problem, before performing any of the operations. This frequently enables a scholar to shorten his work by cancellation, etc. In the case of problems whose solution requires tedious processes, some teachers do not require their pupils to do more than to indicate the operations. It is to be feared that much of the lack of facility in adding, multiplying, etc., found in the pupils of the higher classes is due to this desire to make work pleasant. Instead of becoming more expert in the fundamental operations, scholars in their eighth year frequently add, subtract, multiply, and divide more slowly and less accurately than in their fourth year of school.

Paper vs. Slates. — To the use of slates may be traced very much of the poor work now done in arithmetic. A child that finds the sum of two or more numbers by drawing on his slate the number of strokes represented by each, and then counting the total, will have to adopt some other method if his work is done on material that does not permit the easy obliteration of the tell-tale marks. When the teacher has an opportunity to see the number of attempts made by some of her pupils to obtain the correct quotient figures in a long division example, she may realize the importance of such drills as will enable them to arrive more readily at the correct result.

The unnecessary work now done by many pupils will be very much lessened if they find themselves compelled to dispense with the "rubbing out" they have an opportunity to indulge in when slates are employed. The additional expense caused by the introduction of paper will almost inevitably lead to better results in arithmetic. The arrangement of the work will be looked after; pupils will not be required, nor will they be permitted, to waste material in writing out the operations that can be performed mentally; the least common denominator will be determined by inspection; problems will be shortened by the greater use of cancellation, etc., etc. Better writing of figures and neater arrangement of problems will be likely to accompany the use of material that will be kept by the teacher for the inspection of the school authorities. The endless writing of tables and the long, tedious examples now given to keep troublesome pupils from bothering a teacher that wishes to write up her records, will, to some extent, be discontinued when slates are no longer used.

The Walsh Arithmetics.

IN several important particulars the Walsh Arithmetics mark a departure from the traditional method and arrangement.

1. By the "spiral plan" the *elements* of all the important topics are taken up early in the course, adding to the interest and practical worth of the study.

2. In each case the subject taken up is not exhausted at once, but practice in it is carried on with problems of gradually increasing difficulty throughout the course.

3. Drills in addition, subtraction, multiplication and division of abstract numbers are given at intervals throughout the books of the series, thus insuring in pupils of the upper grades, accuracy and speed in the fundamental processes. This is an important and unique feature.

4. The series contains a larger number of varied and practical *concrete* problems than any other.

5. It is the only series containing drills in securing "approximate answers," — work of great advantage in calling the pupil's attention to the conditions of a problem, and thus giving the power to detect at once the absurdity of any result greatly wide of the mark.

Such obvious merits of the lower book as the alternation of oral, sight and slate work, the early introduction of United States currency (leading to decimals), the easy beginnings with fractions and denominate numbers, and the freshness and interest insured by the great variety of means used to secure perfect mastery of simple number combinations, cannot be too strongly emphasized.

In the higher book we note the wide range of subjects treated in their simple elements, the great variety of practical problems, the early introduction of percentage and simple interest, of bills and receipts, and all the matters connected with simple commercial arithmetic.

Unique features are : the many short methods noted, the use of approximate answers, the abundant drills in the four fundamental processes, and the introduction of algebra in a way so natural and simple that children of ten may easily grasp enough of it to shorten many of the longer arithmetical processes.

The Walsh books illustrate most admirably what every teacher knows so well, that many things that are complex in their completeness, are in their elements simple and easily comprehended by young children.

The series is thoroughly up to the demands of modern pedagogy ; it is inductive in method, practical and varied in treatment, and pursues one object from start to finish, i. e., to make clear thought and accurate computation matters of habit, and to lay the foundation for the intelligent use of mathematical principles.

A comparison of the number of subjects treated in any given one hundred pages of Walsh with a corresponding one hundred pages in any other series makes evident Walsh's superiority both in variety and freshness, and in drill and review upon essentials.

The Heart of Oak Books.

A collection of traditional rhymes and stories for children, and of masterpieces of poetry and prose, for use at school and at home, chosen with special reference to the cultivation of the imagination and a taste for good reading. By

CHARLES ELIOT NORTON.

These six volumes provide an unrivaled means of making good reading more attractive than bad, and of giving right direction to uncritical choice, by offering to the young, without comment or lesson-book apparatus,

SELECTED PORTIONS OF THE BEST LITERATURE, THE VIRTUE OF WHICH HAS BEEN APPROVED BY LONG CONSENT.

The selections are of unusual length, completeness and variety, comprising a very large proportion of poetry, and are adapted to the progressive needs of childhood and youth by a unique principle of selection, grading and arrangement, which makes each volume a unit, and makes the series the first permanent contribution to the body of school reading by a man of letters which children will love and cherish after school-days are over.

THE FINE TASTE AND RARE LITERARY EXPERIENCE AND RESOURCES

of the editor are a guarantee that the series contains nothing but the very best. No author's name or reputation has been potent enough to save from rejection any selection that did not meet the editor's exacting standard in at least three particulars: First, absolute truth to nature (especially nature in America); second, wide, healthy, human interest; third, the highest possible merit in point of literary form. The result, therefore, is a body of reading of extraordinarily trustworthy character. The youth who shall become acquainted with the contents of these volumes will share in the common stock of the intellectual life of the race, and will have the door opened to him of all the vast and noble resources of that life.

FOR HOME USE,

even by children most favored by circumstance, these volumes provide the richest store of thought and music to grow up with and to learn by heart. No happier birthday or Christmas gift can be conceived, especially for children in the country, or remote from libraries and other means of culture, than a set of the Heart of Oak Books. They are a veritable possession forever, and their price puts them within the reach of all.

Descriptive pamphlet giving prefaces, tables of contents, specimen pages, and indexes of authors sent on application.

D. C. HEATH & CO., PUBLISHERS

BOSTON   NEW YORK   ATLANTA   CHICAGO

ENGLISH LANGUAGE.

Hyde's Lessons in English, Book I. For the lower grades. Contains exercises for reproduction, picture lessons, letter writing, *uses* of parts of speech, etc. 40 cts.

Hyde's Lessons in English, Book II. For Grammar schools. Has enough technical grammar for correct use of language. 60 cts.

Hyde's Lessons in English, Book II with Supplement. Has, in addition to the above, 118 pages of technical grammar. 70 cts. Supplement bound alone, 35 cts.

Hyde's Practical English Grammar. For advanced classes in grammar schools and for high schools. 60 cts.

Hyde's Lessons in English, Book II with Practical Grammar. The Practical Grammar and Book II bound together. 80 cts.

Hyde's Derivation of Words. 15 cts.

Penniman's Common Words Difficult to Spell. Graded lists of common words often misspelled. Boards. 25 cts.

Penniman's Prose Dictation Exercises. Short extracts from the best authors. Boards. 30 cts.

Spalding's Problem of Elementary Composition. Suggestions for its solution. Cloth. 45 cts.

Mathews's Outline of English Grammar, with Selections for Practice. The application of principles is made through composition of original sentences. 80 cts.

Buckbee's Primary Word Book. Embraces thorough drills in articulation and in the primary difficulties of spelling and sound. 30 cts.

Sever's Progressive Speller. For use in advanced primary, intermediate, and grammar grades. Gives spelling, pronunciation, definition, and use of words. 30 cts.

Badlam's Suggestive Lessons in Language. Being Part I and Appendix of Suggestive Lessons in Language and Reading. 50 cts.

Smith's Studies in Nature, and Language Lessons. A combination of object lessons with language work. 50 cts. Part I bound separately, 25 cts.

Meiklejohn's English Language. Treats salient features with a master's skill and with the utmost clearness and simplicity. $1.30.

Meiklejohn's English Grammar. Also composition, versification, paraphrasing, etc. For high schools and colleges. 90 cts.

Meiklejohn's History of the English Language. 78 pages. Part III of English Language above, 35 cts.

Williams's Composition and Rhetoric by Practice. For high school and college. Combines the smallest amount of theory with an abundance of practice. Revised edition. $1.00.

Strang's Exercises in English. Examples in Syntax, Accidence, and Style for criticism and correction. 50 cts.

Huffcutt's English in the Preparatory School. Presents advanced methods of teaching English grammar and compositon in the secondary schools. 25 cts.

Woodward's Study of English. From primary school to college. 25 cts.

Genung's Study of Rhetoric. Shows the most practical discipline. 25 cts.

See also our list of books for the study of English Literature.

D. C. HEATH & CO., PUBLISHERS,

BOSTON.   NEW YORK.   CHICAGO.

READING.

Badlam's Suggestive Lessons in Language and Reading. A manual for primary teachers. Plain and practical; being a transcript of work actually done in the school-room. $1.50.

Badlam's Stepping-Stones to Reading.— A Primer. Supplements the 283-page book above. Boards. 30 cts.

Badlam's First Reader. New and valuable word-building exercises, designed to follow the above. Boards. 35 cts.

Bass's Nature Stories for Young Readers: Plant Life. Intended to supplement the first and second reading-books. Boards. 30 cts.

Bass's Nature Stories for Young Readers: Animal Life. Gives lessons on animals and their habits. To follow second reader. Boards. 40 cts.

Firth's Stories of Old Greece. Contains 17 Greek myths adapted for reading in intermediate grades. Illustrated. Boards. 35 cts.

Fuller's Illustrated Primer. Presents the word-method in a very attractive form to the youngest readers. Boards. 30 cts.

Hall's How to Teach Reading. Treats the important question: what children should and should not read. Paper. 25 cts.

Miller's My Saturday Bird Class. Designed for use as a supplementary reader in lower grades or as a text-book of elementary ornithology. Boards. 30 cts.

Norton's Heart of Oak Books. This series is of material from the standard imaginative literature of the English language. It draws freely upon the treasury of favorite stories, poems, and songs with which every child should become familiar, and which have done most to stimulate the fancy and direct the sentiment of the best men and women of the English-speaking race. Book I, 100 pages, 25 cts.; Book II, 142 pages, 35 cts.; Book III, 265 pages, 45 cts.; Book IV, 303 pages, 55 cts.; Book V, 359 pages, 65 cts.; Book VI, 367 pages, 75 cts.

Penniman's School Poetry Book. Gives 73 of the best short poems in the English language. Boards. 35 cts.

Smith's Reading and Speaking. Familiar Talks to those who would speak well in public. 80 cts.

Spear's Leaves and Flowers. Designed for supplementary reading in lower grades or as a text-book of elementary botany. Boards. 30 cts.

Ventura's Mantegazza's Testa. A book to help boys toward a complete self-development. $1.00.

Wright's Nature Reader, No. I. Describes crabs, wasps, spiders, bees, and some univalve mollusks. Boards. 30 cts.

Wright's Nature Reader, No. II. Describes ants, flies, earth-worms, beetles, barnacles and star-fish. Boards. 40 cts.

Wright's Nature Reader, No. III. Has lessons in plant-life, grasshoppers, butterflies, and birds. Boards. 60 cts.

Wright's Nature Reader, No. IV. Has lessons in geology, astronomy, world-life, etc. Boards. 70 cts.

For advanced supplementary reading see our list of books in English Literature.

D. C. HEATH & CO., PUBLISHERS,

BOSTON.   NEW YORK.   CHICAGO.

ELEMENTARY SCIENCE.

Bailey's Grammar School Physics. A series of inductive lessons in the elements of the science. Illustrated. 60 cts.

Ballard's The World of Matter. A guide to the study of chemistry and mineralogy; adapted to the general reader, for use as a text-book or as a guide to the teacher in giving object-lessons. 264 pages. Illustrated. $1.00.

Clark's Practical Methods in Microscopy. Gives in detail descriptions of methods that will lead the careful worker to successful results. 233 pages. Illustrated. $1.60.

Clarke's Astronomical Lantern. Intended to familiarize students with the constellations by comparing them with fac-similes on the lantern face. With seventeen slides, giving twenty-two constellations. $4.50.

Clarke's How to find the Stars. Accompanies the above and helps to an acquaintance with the constellations. 47 pages. Paper. 15 cts.

Guides for Science Teaching. Teachers' aids in the instruction of Natural History classes in the lower grades.
    I.   Hyatt's About Pebbles. 26 pages. Paper. 10 cts.
    II.   Goodale's A Few Common Plants. 61 pages. Paper. 20 cts.
    III. Hyatt's Commercial and other Sponges. Illustrated. 43 pages. Paper. 20 cts.
    IV. Agassiz's First Lessons in Natural History. Illustrated. 64 pages. Paper. 25 cts.
    V.   Hyatt's Corals and Echinoderms. Illustrated. 32 pages. Paper. 30 cts.
    VI. Hyatt's Mollusca. Illustrated. 65 pages. Paper. 30 cts.
    VII. Hyatt's Worms and Crustacea. Illustrated. 68 pages. Paper. 30 cts.
    VIII. Hyatt's Insecta. Illustrated. 324 pages. Cloth. $1.25.
    XII. Crosby's Common Minerals and Rocks. Illustrated. 200 pages. Paper, 40 cts. Cloth, 60 cts.
    XIII. Richard's First Lessons in Minerals. 50 pages. Paper. 10 cts.
    XIV. Bowditch's Physiology. 58 pages. Paper. 20 cts.
    XV. Clapp's 36 Observation Lessons in Minerals. 80 pages. Paper. 30 cts.
    XVI. Phenix's Lessons in Chemistry. 20 cts.
    Pupils' Note-Book to accompany No. 15. 10 cts.

Rice's Science Teaching in the School. With a course of instruction in science for the lower grades. 46 pages. Paper. 25 cts.

Ricks's Natural History Object Lessons. Supplies information on plants and their products, on animals and their uses, and gives specimen lessons. Fully illustrated. 332 pages. $1.50.

Ricks's Object Lessons and How to Give them.
Volume I. Gives lessons for primary grades. 200 pages. 90 cts.
Volume II. Gives lessons for grammar and intermediate grades. 212 pages. 90 cts.

Shaler's First Book in Geology. For high school, or highest class in grammar school. 272 pages. Illustrated. $1.00.

Shaler's Teacher's Methods in Geology. An aid to the teacher of Geology. 74 pages. Paper. 25 cts.

Smith's Studies in Nature. A combination of natural history lessons and language work. 48 pages. Paper. 15 cts.

Sent by mail postpaid on receipt of price. See also our list of books in Science.

D. C. HEATH & CO., PUBLISHERS,

BOSTON, NEW YORK. CHICAGO.

THE WALSH
ARITHMETICS

WHAT THEY ARE AND
WHAT THEY WILL DO
ALSO
WHAT THEY HAVE DONE
AND ARE DOING, TOLD BY
THOSE WHO USE THEM

PUBLISHED BY
D. C. HEATH & COMPANY
BOSTON   NEW YORK   CHICAGO
ATLANTA   SAN FRANCISCO   LONDON

MATHEMATICS FOR COMMON SCHOOLS

**A Graded Course in Arithmetic with
Simple Problems in Algebra
and Geometry**

By JOHN H. WALSH

Associate Superintendent of Schools, Brooklyn

Arranged in Three-Part or Two-Part Series

The Three-Part Series

Elementary Arithmetic.	Cloth.	218 pages.	30 cents
Intermediate Arithmetic.	Cloth.	252 pages.	35 cents
Higher Arithmetic.	Half leather.	365 pages.	65 cents

The Two-Part Series

Primary Arithmetic.	Cloth.	198 pages.	30 cents
Grammar School Arithmetic.	Half leather.	411 pages.	65 cents

In the Two-Part Series the examination papers are omitted, considerably reducing the bulk, but in no way interfering with the completeness of the course.

The Walsh Arithmetics

INSURE	Rapid and Accurate Computation
GIVE	Constant Review without Repetition
CONTAIN	Abundant and Varied Problems
OMIT	Nothing Essential, Everything Else
ARE	Fresh, Well Graded, and Teachable
EMBODY	the Recommendations of the Committee of Ten
AS WELL AS	of the Committee of Fifteen

The Walsh Arithmetics

F OR over twenty years before his series of arithmetics were published John H. Walsh had been a deep and philosophic student, both in and out of the classroom, of the faults of the old system of presenting arithmetic and of the features which should characterize the modern and effective text-book.

How far he had advanced on the right road was shown by the fact that, when the Report of the Committee of Ten was issued, his arithmetics, then in press, were found to have anticipated and practically embodied all the important recommendations of that report. Again, with the recommendations of the Committee of Fifteen, the agreement is quite as close.

These facts show that sound principles underlie the Walsh Arithmetics. Further evidence is that several series of arithmetics have appeared since, built on the same principles, but it is worth noting that no one of these imitators has produced books as faultless as those of Mr. Walsh.

Features of Especial Merit

Division of Work

THE work of this arithmetic is divided into sixteen chapters, each containing a half-year course. The *elements* of all the important topics are taken up early, and treated more fully in each succeeding chapter. Advanced work in all the lines with oral and written drill is given in each chapter with special reviews.

No Unnecessary Rules

CHILDREN learn the quick and accurate working of processes long before they can comprehend the underlying principles, and it is a mistake to misuse valuable time upon the unnecessary memorizing of rules and definitions. True education will stimulate the mental activity of the child by helping him to work out his own rules inductively. He will then stand on his feet securely, and what he knows he will know well. The real educator should be the living teacher; the text-book but an instrument.

The Method of Grading

THE old method was to take up one topic after another, beginning with addition, and to exhaust each one before going on to the next. Under this system many pupils who left school before the end of the course had no knowledge at all of certain subjects which would be of great practical value to them — as percentage, denominate numbers, etc. On the other hand, experience has shown that many graduates cannot add, subtract, multiply, and divide with facility and accuracy, from too little practice during the later years of school life.

Mr. Walsh has taken what may be called "the spiral plan," or, as the French express it, the "concentric circle method." The book is divided, not by topics but by half-year courses. Practice in each subject is carried on with problems of gradually increasing difficulty through the whole course. Drill in the four fundamental processes is found in all the chapters. On the other hand, certain subjects, as mensuration and denominate numbers, are begun much earlier, in simple form, of course, than in other books, so that pupils who do not finish the course will have a much better grasp of the whole subject of arithmetic and be better fitted to apply its principles in the practical business of life.

Great Number of Problems

INCLUDING drill exercises and oral work, there are *over 7600 exercises and problems in the first book alone.* The second book contains a proportionate amount of practice work. No other arithmetic has nearly as many exercises and practical problems. Teachers who use the Walsh Arithmetics do not need to search for extra material to give their classes sufficient practice.

Variety of Problems

EACH problem is unlike the previous one, and will require the pupil to read it carefully. He cannot work it by referring to a "sample" at the head of the page. Variety is also given by the problems in a large number of examination papers from many sources, which are included in the Three-Book Course. Papers are given which have been used in national, state, and municipal civil service examinations, as well as in school and college examinations.

Oral and Sight Work

A GREAT amount of oral work is given all through these books, both under the several topics discussed and in the continuous reviews. The amount and variety of this oral work covers all the ground of a mental arithmetic and answers all the demands for a manual of this subject.

In addition to the usual oral work, practice in *sight work* has been introduced. Problems are put upon the blackboard by the teacher, the pupils perform the necessary processes mentally and write the answers as quickly as possible. This is a helpful form of drill.

Approximate Answers

PRACTICE in approximate answers will prove to be of the greatest practical value, for, in business life, one cannot always stop to reckon with paper and pencil, but must be ready to estimate quickly the approximate result in order to make a decision. By such practice in rapid computation pupils learn to note all conditions of a problem and soon detect at once the absurdity of any result wide of the mark. *This useful drill is found in no other series of arithmetics.*

Continuous Reviews

THERE are not only frequent but continuous reviews, which constantly apply all that has been learned without actual repetition of material previously used. Pupils thus cannot lose their readiness in the application of the simpler and more fundamental processes. Each half-year's work contains its own review chapter and the lessons arranged for this purpose will be especially appreciated by teachers.

Algebra Work

MODERN educational methods, as recommended by the various committees who have made a special study of elementary school problems, all require the introduction of simple algebra work in the grammar grades. The algebra work included in the Walsh Arithmetics, in Chapters X and XV, is within the capacity of the average pupil and sufficiently full to give him all the training which it is desirable for him to have in this grade of work. It perfectly meets the recommendations of the Committee of Ten and the Committee of Fifteen. To enable a teacher unfamiliar with this work to do it successfully, he has only to follow the lines laid down in the manual.

Elementary Geometry

ELEMENTARY Geometry was recommended by the Committee of Ten above referred to and is now generally taught in the upper grammar grades. The chapter on geometry in the Walsh books contains sufficient material for two years' work. Pupils who have mastered the work presented in this chapter will find little difficulty in solving the questions in inventional geometry commonly offered in examination papers.

General Statement

IN the lower book the alternation of oral, sight, and written work, the early introduction of United States currency (leading to decimals), the easy beginnings with fractions and denominate numbers, are advantages which cannot be too strongly emphasized.

In the higher book the range of subjects, the practical problems, the early introduction of percentage and simple interest, of bills and receipts, and all the matter connected with simple commercial arithmetic, together with the short methods for approximate answers, are notable points of superiority.

The series is thoroughly up to the demands of modern pedagogy. It is inductive in method and aims to develop clear thought and the power of accurate computation and to lay the foundation for the intelligent use of mathematical principles.

Weighty Words of Educators

ALBERT LEONARD, *Pres. Mich. Nor. Schools, Ypsilanti, Mich.*

Walsh's Arithmetics embody the best ideas of modern educational philosophy and are a distinct improvement upon the older text-books. I do not know of any better books for school use than this series.

W. V. HAILMAN, *Superintendent, Dayton, Ohio.*

The Walsh Arithmetics are highly satisfactory to me in every respect. They are eminently practical and free from pernicious puzzles. I appreciate the attention which the books pay to the place of arithmetic in mensuration and in industrial pursuits, and the effective manner in which, in the advanced grades, they make the transition to considerations of general arithmetic or algebra.

C. W. CRUIKSHANK, *Superintendent, Fort Madison, Iowa.*

The books are standing the test of the classroom admirably. I find them well graded, am well pleased with the amount of work furnished, and believe that the " Spiral Method " is the correct method. The books require independent work on the part of the pupils. I am growing to like them better as I see the results of their use in our schools.

B. E. JACKSON, *Superintendent, West Superior, Wis.*

The Walsh Arithmetics have been in use in this city for a number of years, and they stand higher in the estimation of the Board, teachers, and patrons of the school than ever before. I consider them the best series published, and heartily endorse the " Spiral Plan " as sound pedagogically.

W. McK. VANCE, *Superintendent, Urbana, Ohio.*

My teachers without exception are earnest admirers and hearty supporters of the spiral plan of teaching arithmetic, as it appears in the Walsh series. The problems are graded with such nicety that the pupil meets every difficulty with an increasing sense of power. I commend the books heartily and without reservation.

I. C. PHILLIPS, *Superintendent, Lewiston, Maine.*

We have used the Walsh Arithmetics for three years. Teachers and pupils are well pleased with them, and the results are better than I have ever obtained with any other series of arithmetics.

W. N. LISTER, *County Com. Schools, Ann Arbor, Mich.*

The Walsh Arithmetics are now in very general use throughout the county and I have yet to hear the first unfavorable criticism from my teachers. On the contrary, they are expressing themselves gratified with the results obtained from the new plan.

S. A. FARNSWORTH, *Principal, St. Paul, Minn.*

Four years ago the Walsh Arithmetics were adopted for the St. Paul schools. When the period of adoption expired last summer, the principals of the forty-five schools of the city were practically unanimous in recommending their continuance. They are eminently adapted to foster careful and accurate reasoning along mathematical lines. A marked improvement has been shown in the subject since we began the use of the books.

C. D. GRAWN, *Prin. Ypsilanti Normal Training School.*

During the twenty years of my experience as a teacher and a superintendent I have never before made use of a series of arithmetics that have enabled us to reach such gratifying results.

The books are well graded, afford frequent opportunities for review, have well-selected and practical exercises, and in the second book of the grammar course give the pupil a good working knowledge of the algebraic equation and an intelligent understanding of the concepts of elementary geometry, both of which features fully comply with the recommendations of the Committee of Ten.

F. S. SUTCLIFFE, *Superintendent, Arlington, Mass.*

I have for two years supervised the work of classes using Walsh Arithmetics, and for definite, reliable results I count them the best books I ever used.

"FULLY A YEAR IN ADVANCE"

ELGIN, ILL.

D. C. HEATH & CO. :

We have been using the Walsh Arithmetics in our schools for several years, and are pleased with the books because of what they have done in making our arithmetic work more efficient. Our pupils are fully a year in advance of what they were when the books were introduced, — grade for grade, I mean.

Permit me to suggest a few of the strong points of these books from the standpoint of teachers who are using them : —

1. A large number of simple problems.

2. Frequent reviews.

3. An abundance of oral work, thus doing away with the necessity for a separate book in mental arithmetic.

4. Early introduction of easy work in fractions, denominate numbers, percentage, and interest.

5. Simple explanation.

6. Distribution of elementary work in algebra and geometrical measurements and constructions so that it may supplement and elucidate the work in arithmetic.

7. Beginning algebra work with equation.

Our teachers find that this work very greatly aids clear thinking and accuracy of statement. I unhesitatingly recommend the books.

M. A. WHITNEY, Supt. of Schools.